To: Mrs. Durkin

From: Kelsey

1999

THE DELECTABLE

APPLE

Text copyright © 1994 by Kathleen Desmond Stang.
Illustrations copyright © by Lynne Riding.

Printed in Hong Kong.

Library of Congress Cataloging-in-Publication Data

Stang, Kathleen Desmond.
      The delectable apple / by Kathleen Desmond Stang.
            p.   cm.
      Includes bibliographical references and index.
      ISBN 0-8118-0524-7
      1. Cookery (Apples)   I. Title.
   TX813.A6S73   1994
   641.6'41—dc20   94-5193
                                          CIP

Cover design: Lynne Riding, Marianne Mitten
Composition: Marianne Mitten

Distributed in Canada by Raincoast Books,
112 East Third Ave., Vancouver, B.C. V5T 1C8

10 9 8 7 6 5 4 3 2 1

Chronicle Books
275 Fifth Street
San Francisco, CA 94103

THE DELECTABLE

APPLE

KATHLEEN DESMOND STANG
ILLUSTRATIONS BY LYNNE RIDING

CHRONICLE BOOKS

SAN FRANCISCO

DEDICATION:

To my father and mother,
Gerald and Virginia Desmond,
who showed me from the very beginning
what really good food is.

And to Bob, the apple of my eye.

ACKNOWLEDGMENTS:

Special thanks to Leslie Jonath, to Susan Derecskey,
and to Dr. Robert A. Norton for his help with the Glossary.

ALSO BY KATHLEEN DESMOND STANG:

A Little Northwest Cookbook

Contents

For as long as I can remember, I've loved apples. The crisp sweet-tart Pippins of childhood picnics. The hefty, red-streaked Liberty first tasted at Seattle's Pike Place Market. And the juicy, white-fleshed McIntosh bought from the back of a battered pickup in Freeport, Maine.

Apples have been popular since Adam and Eve, although the first "apple" may well have been a pomegranate. The apple tree is said to have originated in western Asia, near the Caucasus Mountains. As new varieties developed from chance seedlings, apples spread throughout the world's temperate zones. Both the ancient Egyptians and Romans cultivated apples. Pliny the Elder mentioned dozens of varieties in his *Historica Naturalis*. Now thousands of varieties are known, with twenty-five hundred named apples grown in the United States alone, and the research for new disease-resistant, flavorful varieties continues.

The Pilgrims brought apple seeds and cuttings with them to North America where the trees flourished. John Chapman, known popularly as Johnny Appleseed, traveled throughout western Pennsylvania, Ohio, and Indiana, sowing apple seeds and sometimes apple trees.

The oldest apple tree planted in the Northwest stands near Fort Vancouver, north of Portland and the Columbia River. The seed is thought to have been brought from London around the Horn in 1825 in the coat pocket of a Hudson's Bay Company employee.

The vast irrigated orchards of eastern Washington make Washington State first in commercial sales in the country, followed by New York, Michigan, California, Pennsylvania, and Virginia. Apples, in fact, can be grown in every state in the continental United States and across Canada.

All apples are not alike. A cider apple, for example, won't bake well just as a baking apple, such as Rome Beauty, is generally too dry and mealy to eat out of hand. The Glossary on page 66 indicates which apples are best for baking, sauce, general cooking, and eating out of hand.

Included in this book are some of my favorite apple recipes collected over the years. Apple Strudel demonstrated by an Austrian friend at her kitchen table. Tarte Tatin made by La Varenne's Chef Chambrette in Paris. And, of course, my dad's famous gingerbread with a twist.

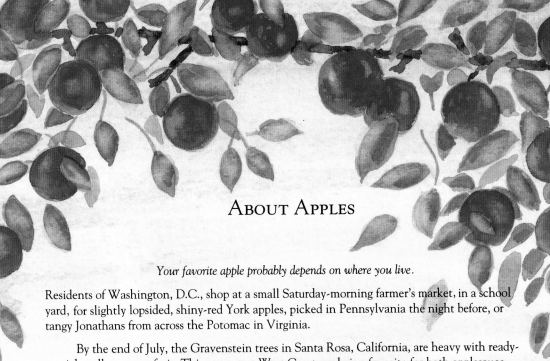

About Apples

Your favorite apple probably depends on where you live.

Residents of Washington, D.C., shop at a small Saturday-morning farmer's market, in a school yard, for slightly lopsided, shiny-red York apples, picked in Pennsylvania the night before, or tangy Jonathans from across the Potomac in Virginia.

By the end of July, the Gravenstein trees in Santa Rosa, California, are heavy with ready-to-pick, yellow-green fruit. This tart-sweet West Coast apple is a favorite for both applesauce and pie.

On crisp autumn weekends in upstate New York, families descend on pick-your-own orchards and roadside farm stands for carloads of juicy, crisp McIntosh and its newer relatives, Macoun and Empire.

On the west side of the Cascade Mountains—from Portland to British Columbia—both old and new varieties thrive in the cool, damp climate. One grower just outside Seattle harvests more than forty varieties from dwarf trees on his three-and-a-half-acre plot. Visitors haul away boxes of small red Akanes and big red-blushed Jonagolds as well as old favorites like Ashmeads Kernel and Twenty-Ounce Pippin.

Along the Columbia, Yakima, and Wenatchee rivers of eastern Washington State, the biggest apple-producing region in the country, the traditional top sellers—Red Delicious, Golden Delicious, and Granny Smith—continue to thrive, but many new varieties are gaining ground. There, and throughout the country, growers are experimenting with new types such as Gala and Braeburn from New Zealand, Fuji and Mutsu (also called Crispin) from Japan, and Liberty and Empire developed here in the United States.

Thousands of years ago, the only way apples grew was from apple seeds, either deliberately planted or windfalls. And, since each seed was different, carrying its own particular characteristics, the chances of an apple seed producing a great apple were limited at best.

Then, about 400 B.C., the Romans discovered how to take a cutting from a favored tree and graft it onto a strong root stock in order to duplicate the original variety. This is the way some of our well-known varieties were propagated. On the other hand, Rome Beauty, McIntosh, Jonathan, Red Delicious, Golden Delicious, and Granny Smith were all discovered as what are called chance seedlings.

In addition to reproducing a variety, plant breeders, in controlled conditions, are also able to cross two known varieties to make a new apple. The vast majority of these crosses have no potential, but occasionally, after twenty to forty years of testing, one will show real promise.

For example, Jonagold, a cross between Jonathan and Golden Delicious, carries some of the characteristics of each parent. Likewise, Empire combines the sweetness of Red Delicious with the tang of a McIntosh.

In the last half century, some plant breeders have concentrated on developing new disease-resistant varieties, ones that are easier to grow, keep well, and taste great, too. One success story from Geneva, New York, is Liberty, a juicy, sweet-tart, good-for-eating, red apple similar to Macoun, one of its parents.

In general, apples can be divided into eating apples (sometimes called dessert apples) and cooking apples. Eating apples are the sweet, crisp varieties, like Gala, Red Delicious, and Criterion, which are low in acid, high in sugar, and tend to become bland when cooked. Cooking apples, on the other hand, are firm and tart, like Rhode Island Greening, York, and

Northern Spy, which are perfect for pies and other culinary uses. Many apples, however, are considered to be all-purpose and can be used successfully for both cooking and eating fresh. Examples are Braeburn, Elstar, Fuji, and Jonagold.

Cooking apples can be further defined by the method of cooking.

A baking apple requires a tender skin and flesh that holds its shape when cooked. Rome Beauty has long been considered the queen of the bakers, but others in this category include Cortland, Melrose, Elstar, Golden Delicious, Idared, Jonagold, Newtown Pippin, Spartan, and Jonathan. The length of time the apple is cooked is also a consideration. The Empire bakes more quickly than others, while the dense Fuji and Melrose take longer than average.

A tart apple is needed for pie, and the slices should maintain their shape when cooked. Candidates for first-rate apple pie include Newtown Pippin, Gravenstein, Northern Spy, Greening, Stayman's Winesap, Winesap, Jonathan, Cortland, Akane, and Idared. Many cooks favor McIntosh, Empire, and Granny Smith for pies, but the slices do tend to fall apart as they cook.

For sauce an entirely different kind of apple is needed—just the opposite than for pie. A sauce apple will disintegrate into a pleasant rough or smooth texture when heated. Add the sugar before cooking for a chunky sauce; stir it in at the end for a smooth one. Gravenstein, Cortland, Empire, McIntosh, and Greening are all excellent sauce apples. For a pretty, pale pink sauce, use a red-skin variety such as Jonathan, Akane, or Idared. Cook the apples with the skins on, then puree them.

These days, apples are a year-round fruit. The season begins, depending on location, in late summer with the harvest of the first early varieties—Galas, Gravensteins, and Akanes—apples high in sugar, often best eaten out-of-hand.

Then, between September and December comes the bulk of the harvest. Hundreds of varieties fill supermarkets and roadside stands. Bins and baskets of green, yellow, and red-striped fruit, plus all those heavily ladened backyard trees. Some varieties are so perishable they are on the stands for only a few weeks. And others are in such limited supply—or so fragile—that they are sold only where they are grown.

Some varieties, like Fuji, are considered keepers, apples that retain their flavor and crispness for a couple of months in a home refrigerator. Other varieties, like Red and Golden Delicious, are held commercially in cold storage or in a low-oxygen environment called controlled atmosphere (CA) for the better part of a year.

Come spring, we benefit from the reversal of the seasons and our markets brim with Braeburns and Galas and Granny Smiths from the Southern Hemisphere.

Apples—any time of year!

BREAKFAST & BREADS

Apple Streusel Coffee Cake

You can start the night before to make this warm, cinnamony breakfast treat. Combine and refrigerate the topping and the liquid ingredients for the batter separately, then sift the dry ingredients. In the morning, it takes only a few minutes to chop the apple and layer the cake.

Streusel topping
½ cup (packed) light brown sugar
¼ cup all-purpose flour
1 teaspoon ground cinnamon
2 tablespoons butter, chilled

Apple batter
1⅓ cups all-purpose flour
½ cup sugar
2 teaspoons baking powder
½ teaspoon salt
½ cup milk
1 egg
¼ cup vegetable oil
1 teaspoon vanilla extract
1 cooking apple, such as Newtown Pippin, Empire, or Macoun, peeled, cored, and
   finely chopped
½ cup finely chopped pecans or almonds

To make topping, combine brown sugar, flour, and cinnamon in a small bowl. With fingers, work in butter until crumbly. Set aside.

To make batter, combine flour, sugar, baking powder, and salt. Set aside. In a large bowl, combine milk, egg, oil, and vanilla and mix well.

Preheat oven to 400 degrees. Grease an 8 x 8 x 2-inch baking dish.

Add dry ingredients to liquid ingredients and stir just until moistened. Gently stir in apple. Spoon half the batter into prepared baking dish, sprinkle with half the streusel topping, and cover with remaining batter. Add nuts to remaining streusel and sprinkle on top. Bake about 30 minutes, or until a wooden pick inserted near the center comes out clean. Cut into squares and serve warm.

Apples are a member of the rose family.
Look closely and you'll see that the five-petal blossom looks like a miniature wild rose.
Cut the fruit across the middle and you'll expose five seed pods.
Some varieties, like Red Delicious, have five knobs on the blossom end.

Apple-Walnut Tea Bread

Makes 1 loaf.

A moist, orange-flavored quick bread studded with chunks of fresh apple and toasted walnuts.

¾ cup coarsely chopped walnuts
2 cups all-purpose flour
1 teaspoon baking powder
1 teaspoon baking soda
½ teaspoon salt
½ cup boiling water
3 tablespoons butter
1 cup sugar
2 tablespoons grated orange peel
⅓ cup orange juice
1 egg, slightly beaten
2 teaspoons vanilla extract
1 medium cooking apple, such as Winesap or Newtown Pippin, peeled, cored, and cut into ¼-inch dice

Preheat oven to 350 degrees.

Place walnuts in a shallow pan and toast 10 minutes, shaking the pan occasionally. Set aside to cool.

Combine flour, baking powder, baking soda, and salt. Set aside.

In a large bowl, pour boiling water over butter and stir until melted. Stir in sugar, orange peel, orange juice, egg, and vanilla. Add flour mixture and stir just until moistened. Gently stir in apple and walnuts. Spoon into a greased 9 x 5 x 3-inch loaf pan.

Bake 60 to 65 minutes, or until a wooden pick inserted near the center comes out clean. Cool in the pan 5 minutes, then unmold onto a rack. Cool before slicing.

Make-Ahead Apple Bran Muffins

Makes about 26 muffins.

The make-ahead convenience of these high-fiber, low-calorie muffins is a blessing when you have house guests, or if you just want to bake a few muffins at a time.

> 1 cup boiling water
> 2 cups whole bran cereal
> 1 cup unprocessed bran flakes or additional bran cereal
> 1¾ cups buttermilk
> ½ cup currants, raisins, or chopped dates
> ½ cup vegetable oil
> ½ cup honey
> 2 eggs, slightly beaten
> 2 medium cooking apples, such as Melrose or York, peeled,
>   cored, and cut into ⅛- to ¼-inch chunks
> 2½ cups all-purpose flour
> 2¾ teaspoons baking soda
> ½ teaspoon salt
> ½ teaspoon ground cinnamon
> ¼ teaspoon ground nutmeg
> Honey (optional)

Pour boiling water over bran cereal and bran flakes in a large bowl. Stir and let stand 5 minutes. Stir in buttermilk, currants, oil, honey, eggs, and apple and mix well. Combine flour, baking soda, salt, cinnamon, and nutmeg. Stir into bran mixture until just combined. (If desired, refrigerate the muffin mix in a tightly covered container for up to 5 days.)

Preheat oven to 400 degrees. Grease as many muffin cups as needed.

Fill cups three-fourths full with batter. Bake about 25 minutes, or until golden brown and cooked through. Serve warm with honey, if desired.

Fresh Apple Waffles
with Cinnamon-Cider Syrup

Makes about 5 (7-inch) round waffles.

We started out married life with an old, well-seasoned waffle iron from my husband's grandmother. Bob's been the family waffle maker ever since. With a glass of milk, these waffles are a healthy breakfast, especially when topped with applesauce or a not-too-sweet Cinnamon-Cider Syrup.

> 1¼ cups all-purpose flour
> ¼ cup whole wheat flour or additional all-purpose flour
> 2 tablespoons (packed) light brown sugar
> 1½ teaspoons baking powder
> ½ teaspoon baking soda
> ½ teaspoon salt
> 2 eggs, separated
> 1½ cups buttermilk
> 3 tablespoons vegetable oil
> 1 medium red apple, such as Braeburn or Jonathan, unpeeled, cored, and finely chopped
> Cinnamon-Cider Syrup (recipe follows) or maple syrup

Combine flours, brown sugar, baking powder, baking soda, and salt. Set aside. Beat egg whites in large bowl of an electric mixer at high speed until stiff peaks form. Transfer to another bowl and set aside. Preheat waffle iron.

In the same large mixer bowl, combine buttermilk, egg yolks, and oil and mix well. On slow speed, gradually beat in the flour mixture until just blended. If the mixture seems too thick, add a spoonful or two of milk. Stir in the apple. Fold in the egg whites.

Brush the waffle iron grids with oil. Spoon about ¾ cup batter per waffle onto the hot waffle iron. Bake about 5 minutes, or until steaming stops. Serve hot with Cinnamon-Cider Syrup or maple syrup.

Cinnamon-Cider Syrup

MAKES 1 CUP.

4 cups apple cider or apple juice
2 tablespoons (packed) light brown sugar
1 cinnamon stick (3 to 4 inches)

Combine cider, brown sugar, and cinnamon stick in a large, heavy saucepan. Cook at a slow boil about 1 hour, or until reduced to 1 cup. Remove and discard cinnamon stick. The syrup will be thin. Serve warm.

NOTE. The syrup can be made ahead and refrigerated. Reheat before serving.

All human history attests
That happiness for man — the hungry sinner! —
Since Eve ate apples, much depends on dinner.

Lord George Noel Gordon Byron,
Don Juan

BAKED APPLE RINGS

This is an easy way to make a big batch of apple rings. Serve them warm from the oven with sausages or over hot oatmeal for breakfast. Or spoon them over vanilla ice cream for dessert. The rings are also used in Pizza with Sausage and Apple Rings (page 40).

½ cup sugar
1 teaspoon ground cinnamon
3 tablespoons melted butter
2 tablespoons lemon juice
4 medium cooking apples, such as Newtown Pippin, Mutsu, or Golden Delicious

Preheat oven to 425 degrees.

Combine sugar and cinnamon in a shallow dish and combine butter and lemon juice in another. Core and peel apples. Trim ends, then slice each apple crosswise into 4 rings about ½ inch thick. Coat each apple ring on both sides with lemon-butter then dip into the cinnamon-sugar to coat both sides.

Arrange closely on a 15 x 10 x ¾-inch baking pan. Bake about 15 minutes, turning once, or until apples are tender and golden brown.

Remove from pan with a spatula and serve warm or use on the pizza.

GIANT CINNAMON ROLLS
WITH APPLE-RAISIN FILLING

MAKES 8 GENEROUS SERVINGS.

A rainy weekend afternoon is an inviting time to make these easy but somewhat time-consuming cinnamon rolls. The leftovers freeze well.

YEAST DOUGH
4¼ to 4¾ cups bread flour
⅓ cup sugar
1 package fast-rising yeast
1 teaspoon ground cinnamon
¾ teaspoon salt
1¼ cups milk
¼ cup (½ stick) butter
2 eggs, slightly beaten

APPLE-RAISIN FILLING
¼ cup (½ stick) butter
3 medium to large cooking apples, such as Empire or Stayman, peeled, cored,
    and cut into ⅓-inch dice
1 cup raisins
1 cup (packed) light brown sugar
2 teaspoons ground cinnamon
Dash salt
1 tablespoon plus 1 teaspoon grated lemon peel
1 teaspoon lemon juice

SUGAR GLAZE
1¼ cups powdered sugar, sifted
1 tablespoon butter, softened
⅛ teaspoon vanilla extract
2 to 3 tablespoons apple juice or milk

To make dough, combine 3 cups of the flour, the sugar, yeast, cinnamon, and salt in large bowl of an electric mixer. Heat milk and butter in a saucepan or microwave to 120 to 130 degrees. Pour over flour mixture and beat 1 minute. Add eggs and beat 2 minutes longer at medium speed. Gradually stir in enough of remaining flour to make a soft dough. Knead with a dough hook or by hand on a floured surface until smooth and elastic. Place in an oiled bowl, cover, and let rise in a warm place until doubled, about 30 to 40 minutes.

To make filling, heat butter in a large skillet. Add apples and sauté until tender, about 10 minutes. Stir in raisins and transfer to a bowl. Add brown sugar, cinnamon, and salt. Stir in lemon peel and juice. Set aside.

Punch down dough and knead briefly on a floured surface. Let rest 10 minutes. Roll and stretch dough to an 18-inch square. Spread with apple filling and roll up jelly-roll fashion. Moisten edge of dough with water and pinch to seal. Cut crosswise into 8 equal slices and arrange, cut side up, in a greased 9 x 13 x 2-inch baking dish. Cover and let rise until almost doubled, about 30 to 40 minutes.

Preheat oven to 375 degrees.

Bake 30 minutes, or until golden brown and dough is cooked when a knife is inserted between rolls. Cool 10 minutes in the baking dish on a rack.

To make glaze, stir together powdered sugar, butter, and vanilla. Add enough apple juice to make a smooth spreading consistency. Drizzle glaze over warm rolls. Serve warm.

Or cool unglazed rolls completely. Reheat, covered loosely with foil, at 300 degrees for 25 minutes, or until thoroughly heated. Drizzle warm rolls with the glaze.

ELLEN'S APPLE FRITTERS

My sister-in-law Ellen learned to make these pancake-like fritters from her Grandmother Bast, who lived next door when she was a little girl in Madison, Wisconsin. Nowadays she uses Gravensteins from her backyard in Sonoma County, California.

> 3 cooking apples, such as Gravenstein or Newtown Pippin
> 1 cup all-purpose flour
> ⅓ cup sugar
> 1 teaspoon baking powder
> ¾ cup milk
> 2 eggs, beaten
> 2 tablespoons melted butter, cooled, plus extra for frying
> Vegetable oil
> Powdered sugar

Quarter, core, peel, and cut the apples crosswise into thin slices. You should have about 5½ cups. Set aside.

Stir together flour, sugar, and baking powder in a large bowl. Combine milk, eggs, and 2 tablespoons melted butter and stir into flour mixture. Add apples and stir just until mixed.

Heat about ½ teaspoon butter and ½ teaspoon oil in a large nonstick skillet or electric frying pan over medium-high heat. When it bubbles, add about ½ cup of the apple batter, making 3 fritters at a time. Cook, turning once, about 2½ to 3 minutes, or until golden brown. Transfer to a platter and keep warm. Continue with remaining batter, adding additional butter and oil as needed. Sprinkle with sugar and serve warm.

NOTE. Leftover fritters can be rewarmed in a microwave oven at medium power for 20 to 30 seconds per fritter.

Salads, Soups & Condiments

Winemaker's Chicken Salad

Take along a colorful chicken salad for a picnic lunch—perhaps at a winery. Pack the chilled salad, lettuce, and a couple of different kinds of apples, then put them together at the site. Don't forget to include some good crusty bread and white wine.

3 to 3½ cups cubed cooked chicken
¾ cup red, green, or black grape halves, seeded if necessary
¾ cup sliced celery
3 tablespoons currants or raisins

Vinaigrette
¼ cup olive oil
2 tablespoons white wine or apple juice
1 tablespoon white wine vinegar
1½ teaspoons honey
1 teaspoon Dijon mustard
¼ teaspoon salt
⅛ teaspoon freshly ground pepper

2 red eating apples, such as Liberty, McIntosh, Spartan, or Macoun, unpeeled
1 head butter lettuce, leaves washed and crisped

Combine chicken, grapes, celery, and currants in a bowl. Combine ingredients for the vinaigrette in a jar with a tight-fitting lid. Shake well and pour over chicken mixture. (Salad can be made ahead to this point and refrigerated for up to 6 hours.)

Cut apples into bite-size pieces, add to salad, and toss gently. Arrange on lettuce-lined plates or platter. Or toss salad with torn lettuce leaves.

Autumn Apple Salad
with Hazelnut Vinaigrette

MAKES 6 TO 8 SERVINGS.

For an extra splash of color and flavor add a few end-of-the-season raspberries. This salad is equally delicious with walnut oil and toasted walnuts.

⅓ cup hazelnut oil or olive oil
2 tablespoons raspberry vinegar
1 tablespoon apple juice
½ teaspoon hot-sweet mustard
¼ teaspoon salt
¼ teaspoon freshly ground black pepper
⅓ cup hazelnuts (filberts) (1½ ounces)
2 eating apples, such as Gala, Braeburn, or Red Delicious, unpeeled
3 cups (lightly packed) butter lettuce, torn into bite-size pieces
2 cups (lightly packed) spinach leaves, torn into bite-size pieces
2 cups (lightly packed) watercress leaves

Combine oil, vinegar, apple juice, mustard, salt, and pepper in a small jar with a tight-fitting lid and shake well. Let stand at room temperature for up to 1 hour.

Preheat oven to 350 degrees.

Place hazelnuts in a shallow pan and toast 10 minutes, shaking the pan occasionally. Transfer nuts to a tea towel and rub off and discard the skins. Cool slightly, then coarsely chop. Set aside.

Quarter, core, and thinly slice apples. Combine with salad greens and nuts in a large salad bowl. Toss lightly. Shake dressing well and pour over salad. Toss again.

Winter Apple Salad
with Fennel and Gorgonzola

Makes 6 to 8 servings.

Reverse the usual order for this dinner-party salad. Mix the dressing with fennel and two kinds of apples in the bottom of a big salad bowl. Layer the greens on top and refrigerate until dinner time. To serve, just add the gorgonzola and toss.

Balsamic Vinaigrette
⅓ cup extra-virgin olive oil
2 tablespoons balsamic vinegar
½ teaspoon salt
¼ teaspoon freshly ground pepper
1 garlic clove, peeled and cut in half

2 eating apples, such as Fuji, Elstar, Cortland, and/or Criterion, unpeeled, cored, and thinly sliced
1 cup diced fennel bulb
3 cups romaine, torn into bite-size pieces
2 cups curly endive, torn into bite-size pieces
2 cups butter lettuce, torn into bite-size pieces
¼ cup crumbled gorgonzola cheese

Combine vinaigrette ingredients in a small jar with a tight-fitting lid. Shake and let stand 20 minutes or refrigerate for up to 2 days. Remove and discard garlic.

Place apples and fennel in the bottom of large salad bowl, add vinaigrette, and toss. Layer the romaine, endive, and butter lettuce on top. Refrigerate, covered with a damp paper towel, for up to 4 hours.

To serve, sprinkle gorgonzola on top and toss thoroughly.

French Squash, Apple, and Leek Soup

Serve this subtly flavored soup in shallow soup plates with a sprinkle of parsley for an elegant first course.

1 tablespoon vegetable oil
1 tablespoon butter
1½ cups sliced leeks, white and pale green part only
½ cup chopped onion
4 cups diced butternut or acorn squash (about 1½ pounds)
2 medium cooking apples, such as Granny Smith or Melrose, peeled, cored, and diced
¼ teaspoon dried thyme
4 cups homemade chicken broth or 2 (14½-ounce) cans chicken broth
¼ cup heavy cream, half-and-half, or light cream
⅛ teaspoon white pepper
Salt
Finely chopped parsley or flat-leaf parsley leaves, for garnish

Heat oil and butter in a large Dutch oven. Add leeks and onion and sauté until soft but not brown, about 5 minutes. Stir in squash, apples, and thyme. Add chicken broth and 1 cup water and bring to a boil. Reduce heat, cover, and simmer until squash and apples are tender, about 30 minutes. Puree, in 1 or 2 batches, in a blender or food processor until smooth. Return to the Dutch oven and add cream, pepper, and salt to taste. Cook over low heat until steaming hot. Ladle into shallow soup plates and garnish with parsley.

A Trio of Applesauces

Chunky Spicy Applesauce

Kris Merritt, whose family grows Gravensteins and Jonagolds in Mount Vernon, Washington, was the inspiration for this easy recipe. It's a great solution if you get carried away picking apples—just double the recipe. The amount of sugar depends on how sweet and how ripe the apples are.

> 3 pounds sauce apples, such as Gravenstein or Jonagold, peeled, cored, and cut into chunks
> ¼ to ½ cup (packed) light brown sugar
> ¼ to ½ teaspoon ground cinnamon
> ⅛ to ¼ teaspoon ground nutmeg
> Dash ground allspice
> ¼ cup raisins or chopped dates (optional)

Combine apples, ½ cup water, and brown sugar in a heavy kettle or Dutch oven. Cook, uncovered, over medium-low heat, stirring frequently, until most of the liquid has evaporated and apples are tender, about 20 minutes. Watch carefully, particularly at the end, to prevent scorching. Add additional water if necessary. Stir in spices to taste and raisins, if desired. Serve warm or chilled.

Pink Ginger Applesauce

Makes about 3 cups.

An old-fashioned crank-type food mill is handy for applesauce, as is an all-in-one mechanism that peels, cores, and slices apples with a few turns of the handle.

3 pounds red sauce apples, such as Winesap, Akane, or York, unpeeled
¾ cup apple juice or water
6 quarter-size slices fresh ginger, peeled
¼ to ½ cup sugar

Quarter the apples, core them, and cut each piece in half crosswise. Combine apple pieces, apple juice, and ginger in a heavy kettle or Dutch oven. Bring to a boil. Reduce heat to a low boil, cover, and cook, stirring occasionally, until apples are mushy, 20 to 45 minutes depending on the density of the apples. Pass through a food mill or coarse strainer and discard apple peels and ginger. Stir in sugar to taste. Serve warm or chilled.

*An apple a day may indeed keep the doctor away.
Virtually devoid of sodium and fat, apples contain carbohydrates, potassium,
and vitamin C, and they are a good source of dietary fiber.
A medium-size apple weighs in at only 80 calories.*

Apple-Horseradish Sauce

Makes about 3 cups.

Serve this tangy sauce with hot roast beef or spread it on cold roast beef and watercress sandwiches.

3 pounds sauce apples, such as Cortland, Spartan, or Granny Smith, peeled, cored, and sliced
¼ cup sugar
4 teaspoons prepared cream-style horseradish
1 teaspoon balsamic vinegar

Place apples in a 2½- to 3-quart microwavesafe casserole. Cover with lid or vented plastic wrap. Microwave at high (100%) about 15 minutes, or until apples are mushy, stirring twice. Let stand, covered, 5 minutes. Stir in sugar, horseradish, and vinegar to taste. Cool.

Note. This recipe can be prepared on the stove top, using the method for Pink Ginger Applesauce (page 30) or for Chunky Spicy Applesauce (page 29). Add about ½ cup water to the apples before cooking.

Select firm, unblemished apples with bright, evenly colored skins.
A warm golden, orange, or red color is a good indication of maturity,

Apple Chutney

This is the sort of relish I associate with a proper British "ploughman's lunch," with chunks of Cheshire cheese, country bread, and a pint of ale. It also complements pork, chicken, and curried dishes.

3 pounds cooking apples, such as Melrose or Jonagold, peeled, cored, and chopped
1 cup minced onion
1¼ cups cider vinegar
1 cup (packed) dark brown sugar
½ cup golden raisins
1 teaspoon ground ginger
1 teaspoon mustard seed
¼ teaspoon salt

Combine all the ingredients in a large kettle or Dutch oven. Bring to a boil. Reduce heat to medium and cook, stirring occasionally, 50 minutes, or until most of the liquid has evaporated. Watch closely at the end to prevent scorching. Spoon into clean glass jars with tight-fitting lids. The chutney can be refrigerated for up to 2 weeks.

ENTRÉES & ACCOMPANIMENTS

Apple and Prune-Stuffed Pork Loin
with Roasted Potatoes

A cross-cultural dish. The apple and prune combination is Danish; the herbs and olive oil, Mediterranean. Serve with Red Cabbage and Apples (page 42).

> 1 (3- to 3½-pound) boneless pork loin roast (see Note)
> Salt and freshly ground pepper
> About 1 teaspoon dried thyme, crumbled, divided in half
> About ½ teaspoon dried rosemary, crumbled, divided in half
> 1 cooking apple, such as Newtown Pippin, Jonagold, or Granny Smith, peeled, cored, and cut into ¼-inch slices
> 8 pitted large prunes
> 2 tablespoons olive oil
> 8 baking potatoes, peeled and cut lengthwise into 4 wedges

For a double top loin roast, cut strings if roast is tied and open the 2 pieces like a book. Sprinkle with salt and pepper and half the herbs. Arrange three-fourths of the apple slices evenly down the center of the roast. Make a row of prunes and spread the remaining apple slices on top. Replace the other section of roast to enclose the filling and tie with heavy string every 2 inches. Sprinkle roast with remaining herbs. Season with salt and pepper.

Preheat oven to 350 degrees.

Heat the olive oil in a large nonstick skillet over medium-high heat. Add roast and brown on all sides, about 12 minutes. Place on a rack coated with cooking spray in a roasting pan. Add potatoes to the same skillet and sauté until brown on all sides. Add to the roasting pan.

Bake for 1 hour 45 minutes, or until internal temperature is 160 degrees for well done. Cover loosely with foil and let stand 10 minutes before slicing. Serve with roasted potatoes.

NOTE. Pork loin is sold in several different forms. For a boned, rolled, and tied pork loin, make a tunnel for stuffing by cutting a 2¼-inch wide slit in the center of each end of the loin. With a long narrow knife, cut through the loin to connect the slits, making an opening about 1¼ inches in diameter. Sprinkle the cavity with salt, pepper, and herbs and fill the pocket from both ends with apples and prunes, spacing evenly.

Keep apples cool.
Store in plastic bags in the refrigerator.
If left at room temperature, apples continue to ripen and lose
their crispness ten times faster than in the refrigerator.

Herb and Apple-Filled Chicken Breast Rolls

Makes 4 servings.

What's for dinner? These simple, low-calorie, make-ahead chicken rolls are perfect for family or company. They even freeze well.

4 skinless, boneless chicken breast halves (about 1 pound)
½ cup finely chopped peeled cooking apple, such as Fuji or York
½ cup soft whole wheat bread crumbs (1 slice)
¼ cup minced mixed fresh herbs, such as equal parts parsley, basil, thyme, oregano, and about 1 teaspoon rosemary
2 tablespoons finely chopped green onion
⅛ teaspoon salt
⅛ teaspoon pepper
About 1 tablespoon light or regular sour cream or plain yogurt
1 teaspoon oil
Fresh apple slices, for garnish
Fresh herb sprigs, for garnish

Pound chicken between moistened plastic wrap until ¼ inch thick. Combine apple, bread crumbs, herbs, green onion, salt, and pepper in a bowl and mix well. Stir in sour cream. Place chicken breasts on a flat surface and divide herb mixture evenly over the surface. Roll up, starting at a narrow end, and place, seam side down, in a greased baking dish. (The chicken rolls can be wrapped well and frozen at this point. Thaw in the refrigerator before cooking.)

Preheat oven to 350 degrees.

Brush rolls with oil and bake about 30 minutes, or until cooked through. With a serrated knife, cut into ⅓-inch slices and serve warm with any drippings spooned over the top. Or chill and slice just before serving. Garnish plates or platter with apple slices and herbs.

NOTE. Recipe can be doubled or tripled.

VEAL MEDALLIONS WITH APPLES
AND APPLE BRANDY SAUCE

MAKES 4 SERVINGS.

Swiss-born Kaspar Donier, chef-owner of Kaspar's by the Bay in Seattle, teams veal—or pork—with apples, giving a Northwest twist to the French classic, Veal Normandy. He recommends using Oregon apple brandy for the dish and serving a Washington State Sémillon with it.

> 4 cooking or all-purpose apples, such as Jonagold, Idared, Granny Smith, or Golden Delicious
> 2 tablespoons sugar
> 1 pound veal or pork tenderloin or loin, cut into 12 to 16 pieces, about ½ inch thick
> Salt and pepper
> About 1 tablespoon vegetable oil
> 2 medium shallots, minced
> 3 tablespoons apple brandy, Calvados, or brandy
> ⅓ cup dry white wine, such as Sémillon
> ⅔ to 1 cup heavy cream
> 2 tablespoons minced parsley
> Grated nutmeg
> Parsley sprigs, for garnish

Peel and core apples. Trim ends and cut each crosswise into 4 rings. Sprinkle on both sides with sugar. Heat a large nonstick skillet over medium-high heat. Add half the apples and fry on both sides until caramelized, about 10 minutes. Remove from skillet, cover, and keep warm. Repeat with remaining apples.

Season veal with salt and pepper. Heat 1½ teaspoons oil in the same skillet. Add only the amount of veal that fits easily in the pan and sauté quickly on both sides just until cooked. Remove and keep warm while cooking remaining veal, adding additional oil as needed. Add to reserved veal.

Reduce the heat to medium. Add shallots to the drippings in the skillet. Sauté over medium heat until tender, about 1 minute. Add the apple brandy, carefully light with a match, and flame. When extinguished, add wine. Bring to a slow boil and reduce by half. Add the cream and cook over medium-high heat until slightly thickened. Stir in the minced parsley and season to taste with nutmeg. Return veal and any juices to the pan and keep warm.

Divide the apple slices among 4 warm dinner plates and arrange the veal medallions and sauce overlapping the apples. Garnish with parsley sprigs. Serve immediately.

Cut apples in equal size pieces to insure even cooking.
An apple corer-peeler-slicer and other such devices can shorten preparation time.

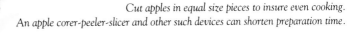

Pizza with Italian Sausage and Apple Rings

MAKES 1 (15-INCH) PIZZA.

Company coming? Try this show-off pizza. We also like it for brunch.

PIZZA DOUGH
2¼ to 2¾ cups all-purpose flour
½ cup whole wheat flour
1 package fast-rising yeast
¾ teaspoon salt
1 cup very warm water (120 to 130 degrees)
2 tablespoons olive oil

TOPPING
⅓ to ½ pound Italian sausage, hot or sweet
½ red onion, thinly sliced
¼ teaspoon fennel or anise seed
¼ teaspoon freshly ground pepper
1 tablespoon cornmeal
3 ounces shredded gouda cheese (1¼ cups)
1 recipe Baked Apple Rings (page 19)

To make the dough, in a large bowl, combine 1½ cups of the all-purpose flour, the whole wheat flour, yeast, and salt. Add water and oil and mix well. Gradually add enough of the remaining flour to make a soft dough. Knead on a lightly floured surface until smooth and elastic. Cover with a cloth and let rest 10 to 30 minutes.

For the topping, remove sausage from casing and crumble into a nonstick skillet. Cook over medium-high heat for 2 minutes. Add onion, fennel seed, and pepper. Sauté until sausage is no longer pink and onion is tender. Transfer to a bowl.

Preheat oven to 400 degrees. Sprinkle a 15-inch pizza pan with cornmeal.

Punch down dough and roll it out to fit the pan. Sprinkle with cheese and arrange apple rings in a decorative pattern. Top with sausage mixture. Bake about 30 minutes, or until crust is golden brown.

An apple by any other name

Dutch *appel*	German *Apfel*	Spanish *manzana*	Finnish *omena*
Indonesian *apel*	French *pomme*	Portuguese *maçà*	Persian *seb*
Swedish *apel*	Catalan *poma*	Greek *melon*	Hindi *sev*
Norwegian *apal*	Latin *malum*	Hungarian *alma*	Japanese *ringo*
Danish *aeble*	Italian *mela*	Turkish *elma*	Chinese *ping guo*

Red Cabbage and Apples

Sweet-and-sour red cabbage is popular throughout Scandinavia. This version, with lots of tart apple slices, is super simple and it tastes even better the second day.

    2 tablespoons butter
    ⅓ cup finely chopped onion
    3 tart cooking apples, such as Rhode Island Greening, Northern Spy, or Jonagold, peeled, cored, and thinly sliced
    3 tablespoons (packed) light brown sugar
    1 teaspoon salt
    1 small red cabbage, quartered, cored, and thinly sliced (about 1½ pounds)
    1 cup dry red wine
    ¼ cup red wine vinegar

Heat butter in a large nonreactive casserole. Add onion and sauté 2 minutes. Stir in apples and sauté 2 minutes. Stir in brown sugar and salt. Add cabbage and toss well. Pour in wine and vinegar. Bring to a boil. Reduce heat and partially cover. Simmer, stirring occasionally, 1½ to 2 hours, or until cabbage and apples are tender. If excessive liquid remains, cook, uncovered, at a slow boil until most has evaporated.

*Two large or three medium apples equal about one pound
or about three cups sliced apples,
two and a half cups diced apples,
or two and a quarter cups finely chopped apples.*

Desserts

All-American Apple Pie

Makes 1 (9-inch) pie.

My youngest sister, Patricia, is famous for her fabulous apple pie. Of course, living across the street from an apple orchard does help. She personalizes each pie with the initials of the guests of honor, but often they're S and T for my niece and nephew, Stephanie and Thomas.

Flaky pastry
2¼ cups all-purpose flour
½ teaspoon salt
¾ cup soft margarine or shortening
4 to 5 tablespoons ice water

Apple filling
3 pounds pie apples, such as Gravenstein, Newtown Pippin, Elstar, or Rhode Island Greening (about 6 apples)
¾ cup sugar
2 tablespoons and 1½ teaspoons cornstarch
1¼ teaspoons ground cinnamon
¼ teaspoon ground ginger
2 tablespoons butter

Vanilla ice cream (optional)
Cheddar cheese (optional)

To make the pastry, combine flour and salt in a bowl. Cut in margarine until mixture is crumbly, the size of small peas. Gradually sprinkle in water, 1 tablespoon at a time, until mixture holds together when gathered with a fork. Press together into two disks, wrap in plastic wrap, and refrigerate 20 minutes, while preparing the fruit, or up to 24 hours. If made ahead, allow the pastry to stand at room temperature 30 minutes before rolling.

To prepare the filling, peel, core, and thinly slice the apples. (You should have about 8 cups.) Combine sugar, cornstarch, cinnamon, and ginger in a bowl and mix well. Add the apples and toss to coat evenly.

Preheat oven to 425 degrees.

Roll out 1 pastry disk on a lightly floured surface to an 11-inch circle. Gently fold in quarters and transfer to a 9-inch pie plate. Unfold and trim crust allowing a 1-inch overhang. Fill with apple mixture and dot with butter. Roll out second pastry disk, fold, and place over fruit. Gently unfold and trim top to ½ inch. Fold lower pastry up over top pastry and crimp to seal. With a narrow, sharp knife cut initials to provide steam vents.

Place pie plate on a pizza pan or baking sheet to catch drips and loosely wrap edges with strips of foil to prevent over-browning. Bake 35 minutes, then remove foil. Continue to bake for a total of 50 to 60 minutes, or until crust is brown and apples are tender. Cool 10 minutes on a rack. Serve warm or at room temperature, with a scoop of vanilla ice cream or a wedge of cheese, if desired.

A squeeze of lemon juice will perk up tired, end-of-season apples for pies and crisps.

ALMOND-APPLE TART

Apples and almonds are a traditional Scandinavian duo. This tart is reminiscent of one we bought in a small shop in downtown Göteborg, Sweden.

PRESS-IN PASTRY
1½ cups all-purpose flour
3 tablespoons sugar
¾ teaspoon grated lemon peel
6 tablespoons (¾ stick) chilled butter, cut into small pieces
1 egg

ALMOND-APPLE FILLING
2 eggs, separated
⅓ cup almond paste (3 ounces)
1 tablespoon plus 1 teaspoon all-purpose flour
1 tablespoon plus 1 teaspoon brandy or milk
2 tablespoons sugar
2½ cooking apples, such as Golden Delicious, Mutsu, or Granny Smith, cored, peeled, and thinly sliced
½ cup sliced almonds (1¼ ounces)

Preheat oven to 350 degrees.

For the pastry, combine flour, sugar, and lemon peel in a bowl. Cut in butter with a pastry blender or rub together with fingers until crumbly. Add egg and stir thoroughly. Shape the mixture into a ball. Press evenly on the sides and bottom of a 10-inch tart pan with a removable bottom. Bake 20 minutes, or until pale golden and firm. Cool.

For the filling, combine egg yolks, almond paste, flour, and brandy in a large bowl. Mix well. Beat egg whites until soft peaks form, gradually beat in the sugar, and continue to beat until barely stiff, not dry. Fold into the almond paste mixture. Arrange the apple slices in concentric circles in the baked shell. Spread the almond filling over the apples and sprinkle with almonds. Bake 45 to 50 minutes, or until golden brown and a knife inserted near the center comes out clean. Cool 10 minutes on a rack and remove the ring. Cool completely before serving.

To prevent cut apples from browning,
coat with lemon juice or drop the slices into lemon water
(one quart water mixed with one tablespoon lemon juice).

Chef Chambrette's Tarte Tatin

Makes 8 servings.

Chef Fernand Chambrette, teaching chef at the École de Cuisine La Varenne in Paris for many years, would say, in French of course, "Add a centimeter of sugar to the pan, then thin slices of butter and as many apples as fit…." Debbie Orrill, who was head stagiairè (apprentice) at the school for a year, translated his recipe into English, converted the crust measurements from metric, and taught me the tricks for this caramelized apple tart. There are beautiful copper pans made especially for this tart, but I find my old 10-inch cast-iron skillet works just fine.

Sweet pie pastry (*PÂTE SUCRÉE*)
2 cups flour
½ cup (1 stick) cold butter, cut into small pieces
½ cup powdered sugar
1 egg

Caramelized apples
½ cup (one stick) cold butter
1¼ cups granulated sugar
7 medium cooking apples, such as Golden Delicious
Whipped cream or crème fraîche

For the pastry, place the flour and butter in the bowl of a food processor fitted with a knife blade. Pulse on and off just until the mixture resembles coarse crumbs. Add the powdered sugar and pulse just to incorporate. Add the egg and pulse to incorporate; do not overprocess. Transfer the mixture, still crumbly, to a bowl and press into a ball; it should be soft but not sticky. Wrap in wax paper or plastic wrap and refrigerate about 30 minutes.

For the apples, butter a skillet with high sides and a heavy base or a round flameproof mold, 10 to 11 inches in diameter. Spread the sugar evenly in the pan. Cut the butter into thin slices and place evenly over the sugar. Peel, halve, and core the apples and arrange, core side up, overlapping on an angle as necessary, to fill the pan. Place over medium heat and cook about 25 minutes, or until the undersides of the apples are caramelized. Rotate the apples in place to caramelize all sides and continue to cook until an amber caramel is formed, 45 to 60 minutes total. Watch carefully near the end so it doesn't burn. Cool on a rack 15 minutes.

Preheat oven to 400 degrees.

Roll out chilled dough on a lightly floured surface to a scant ¼ inch thick. Cut dough a little larger than the pan, place over apples and tuck under edge. (Reserve extra pastry for other uses.) Cut several steam vents in the dough.

Place tart in the oven and reduce heat to 375 degrees. Bake until the crust is golden brown, about 35 minutes. Remove from oven and immediately turn tart out onto a heatproof serving platter. If any of the apples stick to the bottom of the pan, remove them with a spatula and replace on the tart. The tart can be baked several hours ahead and kept at room temperature. Serve it, preferably warm, with whipped cream or crème fraîche on the side.

A word fitly spoken is like apples of gold in pictures of silver.
Proverbs 25:11

Apple Pithiviers

I learned to make a classic pithiviers with real puff pastry in Paris. But, since my French pronunciation is so poor, I have to remind myself to say the four letters P,T,V,A. This is a streamlined version.

4 large cooking apples, such as Melrose, Empire, or Newtown Pippin, peeled, cored, and cut into ¼-inch slices
1 tablespoon butter plus ¼ cup (½ stick) butter, softened
3 tablespoons plus ½ cup sugar
2 eggs
¾ cup ground blanched almonds (3½ ounces)
1 tablespoon all-purpose flour
1 tablespoon apple brandy or brandy
⅛ teaspoon almond extract
1 (17¼-ounce) package frozen puff pastry sheets, thawed according to package directions
1 egg, beaten with 1 tablespoon water, for glaze

Preheat oven to 400 degrees.

Place apples in overlapping layers in a 9 x 13 x 2-inch glass baking pan. Dot with 1 tablespoon of the butter, cut into bits. Sprinkle with 3 tablespoons of the sugar. Bake for 15 minutes, turn apples over, and bake about 10 minutes more, or until tender. (Or microwave on high (100%) for 4 minutes, or until tender.) Cool.

Cream together the remaining ¼ cup butter and remaining ½ cup sugar until fluffy. Add eggs, one at a time, beating well after each. Stir in almonds, flour, brandy, and almond extract.

Roll out 1 pastry sheet on a lightly floured surface into a 12-inch square. Using a pan lid as a guide, cut a 12-inch circle. Transfer to a baking sheet or pizza pan. Spread half of the almond mixture over pastry, leaving a 1-inch border around edge. Arrange apples in overlapping layers on top. Spread with remaining almond mixture. Brush border with glaze.

Roll out remaining pastry to a 14-inch square and cut a 14-inch circle. Arrange over apples. With a pastry cutter, trim edges even and press together with your thumb. With a table knife, push in the edge every ½ inch to form a scalloped design. Cut a small hole in the center. Make about 30 curved slashes, about ⅛ inch from the center to the edge, to form a spiral decoration like a pinwheel. Brush with glaze.

Bake about 25 minutes, or until golden brown. Serve warm.

So-called dessert apples can be just that.
Tart varieties pair nicely with creamy cheeses
such as brie, camembert, and triple cream.
Sweeter apples complement gorgonzola, Roquefort, and other blue cheeses.
Serve the cheese at room temperature and the apples slightly chilled.
Provide fruit knives and forks, if you like.

APPLE-RAISIN SPICE CAKE
WITH BUTTERMILK GLAZE

MAKES ABOUT 12 SERVINGS.

Shredded or finely chopped apples, when added to baked goods, provide additional moisture and help keep them fresh as in this cake for a crowd.

½ cup (1 stick) butter, softened
1 cup sugar
½ cup (packed) light brown sugar
2 eggs
2 cups all-purpose flour
¾ teaspoon baking powder
¾ teaspoon baking soda
¼ teaspoon salt
1 teaspoon ground cinnamon
½ teaspoon ground cloves
¼ teaspoon ground allspice
¼ teaspoon ground ginger
¾ cup buttermilk
1 cup shredded peeled cooking apple, such as Winesap or Gravenstein
1 cup raisins

BUTTERMILK GLAZE
1 cup sugar
½ cup buttermilk
3 tablespoons light corn syrup
¼ cup (½ stick) butter, cut into pieces
½ teaspoon baking soda
2 teaspoons vanilla extract

Preheat oven to 350 degrees.

Cream together the butter, sugar, and brown sugar until light. Add eggs and beat well. Combine the flour, baking powder, baking soda, salt, cinnamon, cloves, allspice, and ginger. Add to butter mixture alternately with buttermilk, beginning and ending with flour mixture. Stir in apple and raisins. Spoon into a greased 9 x 13 x 2-inch pan. Bake about 40 minutes, or until a wooden pick inserted near the center comes out clean. Place on a rack to cool.

For the glaze, combine sugar, buttermilk, corn syrup, and butter in a large saucepan. Bring to a boil, stirring frequently, and cook 4 minutes. Stir in the baking soda and continue to cook 1 minute longer. Remove from the heat and add vanilla. Pour warm glaze over warm or cool cake. Cool completely. Cut into squares to serve.

An apple pie without some cheese
is like a kiss without a squeeze.

PROVERB

Chunky Apple Cake
with Warm Caramel Sauce

Makes about 12 servings.

This rich cake serves twelve elegantly. It is very nice without the caramel sauce, but I've always been one to gild the lily.

> 2 medium to large cooking apples, such as Newtown Pippin or Cortland
> 2 teaspoons grated lemon peel
> 1 tablespoon plus 1 teaspoon lemon juice
> 1 cup (2 sticks) butter, softened
> 2 cups sugar
> 3 eggs
> 1 tablespoon vanilla extract
> 3 cups all-purpose flour
> 1½ teaspoons baking soda
> ½ teaspoon salt
> 1 cup coarsely chopped pecans (about 4 ounces)
> Warm Caramel Sauce (recipe follows)

Peel, core, and finely chop apples. Combine with lemon peel and lemon juice in a bowl.

Preheat oven to 325 degrees.

Cream the butter in large bowl of an electric mixer. Gradually beat in sugar. Add eggs, one at a time, and the vanilla. Combine flour, baking soda, and salt and stir into egg mixture. Stir in the apples and nuts. Spoon the batter into a greased and floured 10-inch tube pan.

Bake 1 hour 15 minutes, or until the cake begins to pull away from the sides of the pan and a wooden pick inserted near the center comes out clean. Cool 10 minutes on a rack and unmold. Serve warm or at room temperature with caramel sauce.

Warm Caramel Sauce

1 cup sugar
¾ cup heavy cream
1 tablespoon butter

Combine the sugar and ½ cup water in a heavy saucepan. Bring to a boil over medium-high heat. Boil, without stirring, until the syrup turns amber, about 15 minutes. Do not allow it to turn dark brown or it will turn bitter. Remove pan from the heat and cool 2 minutes. Carefully pour in cream and stir in butter. Return pan to heat and cook and stir until smooth, about 1 minute. Serve warm.

Note. The caramel sauce can be cooled and refrigerated for up to 1 week. Reheat slowly over low heat or in a microwave oven before serving.

Cinnamon Apple Ice Cream

Makes about 1½ quarts.

Luckily apples are a year-round fruit, so you can serve this ice cream midwinter or on a hot summer day. Soften slightly before serving.

> 2 cooking apples, such as Granny Smith, Fuji, or Akane, peeled, cored, and finely chopped
> ¼ to ½ cup apple juice or cider
> ⅛ teaspoon ground cinnamon
> Dash freshly ground nutmeg
> 4 egg yolks
> ⅔ cup sugar
> 3½ cups half-and-half or light cream
> 1 teaspoon vanilla extract

Combine apples and ¼ cup apple juice in a saucepan. Cook over medium heat, stirring occasionally, until tender and most of the liquid has evaporated. This will take 8 to 15 minutes, depending on the density of the apples. Add more apple juice as needed. Mash the apples with a fork and stir in cinnamon and nutmeg. Transfer to a bowl and set aside.

Whisk together egg yolks and sugar in a large bowl. Heat half-and-half in a large saucepan over medium-high heat until bubbles form around the edge, about 5 minutes. Gradually pour into the egg mixture, stirring constantly. Return the mixture to the saucepan. Reduce the heat to medium-low and cook, stirring, just until the mixture thickens and coats the back of a spoon, about 5 minutes. Do not overheat or the custard will curdle. Strain into a bowl and stir in vanilla and the apple mixture. Chill thoroughly. Freeze in an ice-cream maker according to manufacturer's directions.

Note. Recipe can be halved.

DADDY'S GINGERBREAD WITH APPLES

MAKES 12 SERVINGS.

Gingerbread was my dad's culinary specialty. He'd bake a double recipe in the big roasting pan and serve it in warm slabs spread with butter. His secret recipe, it turns out, was suspiciously like the one that used to be on the bottle of a certain brand of molasses.

½ cup (1 stick) butter, divided

¼ cup (packed) light brown sugar

2 medium cooking apples, such as Newtown Pippin or Rhode Island Greening, peeled, cored, and thinly sliced

⅓ cup sugar

1 egg

1 cup dark molasses

½ teaspoon minced fresh ginger

2½ cups all-purpose flour

1½ teaspoons baking soda

½ teaspoon salt

1 teaspoon ground ginger

1 teaspoon ground cinnamon

½ teaspoon ground cloves

1 cup hot water

Preheat oven to 350 degrees.

Place ¼ cup of the butter and the brown sugar in a 9 x 13 x 2-inch pan. Put in the oven to melt, about 5 minutes. Coat apples in the butter-sugar mixture and arrange in 3 lengthwise rows. Bake 15 minutes.

Meanwhile, cream the remaining butter and the sugar with an electric mixer until fluffy. Add the egg, molasses, and fresh ginger and mix well. Combine flour, baking soda, salt, ground ginger, cinnamon, and cloves. Beating at low speed, add to molasses mixture alternately with hot water, beginning and ending with flour mixture. Pour evenly over apples in the pan. Bake 35 to 40 minutes, or until a wooden pick inserted near the center comes out clean. Cool in the pan 10 minutes. Invert onto a serving tray. Cut into squares and serve warm or at room temperature.

The friendly cow all red and white,
I love with all my heart:
She gives me cream with all her might,
To eat with apple tart.

ROBERT LOUIS STEVENSON
"The Cow"

Italian Apple Cornmeal Cake

Makes 8 servings.

Cornmeal adds a pleasant chewiness to this not-too-sweet cake. Serve with afternoon tea or Florentine style, with cappuccino or a small glass of sweet wine.

> 2 tablespoons plus ¼ cup (½ stick) butter, softened
> 4 tablespoons granulated sugar, divided
> 1 large cooking apple, such as Jonagold, Criterion, or Braeburn
> ¼ cup plain yogurt
> 2 cups sifted powdered sugar
> 2 eggs
> 1 teaspoon vanilla extract
> 1 cup sifted cake flour
> ¼ cup yellow cornmeal
> ¾ teaspoon baking powder
> ½ teaspoon salt

Preheat oven to 350 degrees.

Place 2 tablespoons of the butter in a greased 9-inch cake pan. Heat in oven 5 minutes, or until melted. Sprinkle with 2 tablespoons of the granulated sugar. Peel, core, and cut the apple in half. Thinly slice crosswise into half circles. Arrange apple slices, slightly overlapping, in pan and sprinkle with remaining granulated sugar. Set aside.

Combine the remaining butter, the yogurt, and powdered sugar in a bowl. Beat with an electric mixer until creamy. Beat in the eggs and vanilla. Stir together the flour, cornmeal, baking powder, and salt. Add to the butter mixture in 3 parts, beating well after each addition. Pour the batter over the apples.

Bake about 50 minutes, or until top is golden and a wooden pick inserted near the center comes out clean. Cool 5 minutes on a rack. Loosen edges and invert onto a serving plate. Serve slightly warm or cool completely. Cut into wedges to serve.

Apple Crisp

MAKES 6 TO 8 SERVINGS.

This homey recipe takes advantage of two of Michigan's specialties: apples, particularly Jonathans, and cherries. Since the two seasons do not coincide, I've substituted sweet-tart dried cherries for the fresh.

5½ to 6 cups peeled, cored, and thinly sliced cooking apples, such as Idared,
    Northern Spy, or Jonathan
½ cup dried cherries or dried cranberries
¾ cup all-purpose flour
¾ cup (packed) light brown sugar
¼ teaspoon salt
1 teaspoon ground cinnamon
¼ teaspoon ground nutmeg
½ cup (1 stick) butter, chilled
Vanilla ice cream (optional)

Preheat oven to 350 degrees.

Place apples, dried cherries, and ¼ cup water in a greased 1½- to 2-quart baking dish. Combine flour, brown sugar, salt, cinnamon, and nutmeg in a bowl. Cut in butter until crumbly. Sprinkle over the apples. Cover with lid or foil and bake 30 minutes. Uncover and bake 30 minutes more, or until topping is crisp and apples are tender. Serve warm, at room temperature, or cold, with a scoop of vanilla ice cream, if desired.

Apple-Hazelnut Strudel

MAKES ABOUT 12 SERVINGS.

My Austrian friend, Ingrid Fischmeister, taught me how to make wonderful, authentic strudel. Using the backs of her hands, she stretched the fragile dough until it was nearly transparent. Here the filling recreates her original recipe, but storebought phyllo leaves are used in place of the time-consuming homemade dough. In Austria, this would definitely be served "mit Schlag."

½ cup hazelnuts (filberts) (2½ ounces)
¼ cup (½ stick) plus 5 tablespoons melted butter
½ cup fine dry bread crumbs
4 cooking apples, such as Newtown Pippin or Northern Spy, peeled, cored, and thinly sliced (6 to 7 cups)
½ cup chopped dried apricots
½ cup golden raisins
⅓ cup sugar plus extra for sprinkling on strudels
¼ cup (packed) light brown sugar
½ teaspoon grated lemon peel
1 teaspoon lemon juice
12 sheets (17 x 12-inch) phyllo dough, thawed according to package directions
Softly whipped cream (optional)

Preheat oven to 375 degrees.

Place hazelnuts in a shallow pan and toast 8 minutes, shaking the pan occasionally. Transfer the nuts to a tea towel and rub off and discard the skins. Cool slightly and process in a food processor until finely chopped. Heat ¼ cup butter in a small skillet. Add hazelnuts and bread crumbs and sauté 5 minutes. Set aside.

Combine apples, apricots, raisins, sugar, brown sugar, lemon peel, and lemon juice in a bowl. Mix well and set aside.

Place phyllo sheets between 2 pieces of plastic wrap and cover with a damp tea towel. Carefully transfer 2 sheets to an 18-inch piece of plastic wrap. Brush with melted butter and sprinkle with ⅙ of crumb mixture. Add 2 more sheets, brush with butter, and sprinkle with crumbs. Repeat to make a 6-sheet pile. Arrange half the apple mixture in a row along the short side of the phyllo, starting about 3 inches in from the edge. Using the plastic wrap to start, roll up the phyllo around the filling. Transfer to a large greased baking sheet. Repeat to make a second strudel. Brush the strudels with butter and sprinkle with sugar.

Bake 30 to 35 minutes, or until golden and apples are tender. Cool on the pan 10 minutes. Cut with a serrated knife and serve warm. Garnish with softly whipped cream on the side, if desired.

NOTE. The strudels can be held for 1 day at room temperature, loosely covered. Reheat, covered loosely with foil, at 400 degrees for 15 minutes.

Remember Johnny Appleseed,
All ye who love the apple;
He served his kind by word and deed,
In God's grand greenwood chapel.

WILLIAM HENRY VENABLE
"Johnny Appleseed"

Double Cranberry Baked Apples

Makes 6 servings.

Baked apples may be considered an ordinary dessert, but these—filled with cranberries and cranberry juice and topped with Grand Marnier-whipped cream—are something special.

6 baking apples, such as Melrose, Rome Beauty, or Cortland
⅔ cup chopped fresh or frozen cranberries
¼ cup (packed) light brown sugar
1 teaspoon grated orange peel
¾ cup cranberry juice cocktail
2 tablespoons melted butter
2 tablespoons honey
½ cup heavy cream
1 tablespoon Grand Marnier or other orange liqueur or cranberry juice cocktail
1 tablespoon sugar

Preheat oven to 350 degrees.

Peel top third of each apple. Remove core to within ¼ inch of bottom and enough of pulp so each apple will hold about 2 tablespoons filling. Place apples in a shallow baking dish.

In a small bowl, combine cranberries, brown sugar, and orange peel. Spoon into apples, dividing equally. Whisk together cranberry juice cocktail, melted butter, and honey and pour over apples. Cover with foil and bake 45 minutes. Uncover and bake about 20 minutes more, or until tender, basting occasionally. Beat cream until stiff. Fold in liqueur and sugar. Serve apples warm or at room temperature, garnished with whipped cream.

NOTE. This recipe can be prepared in the microwave. Fill apples as directed and place in a microwavesafe casserole or baking dish. Use only ⅓ cup cranberry juice cocktail and combine with butter and honey in a 2-cup glass measure. Microwave at high (100%) for 30 seconds. Pour over apples and cover with lid or vented plastic wrap. Microwave at high 13 to 15 minutes, or until tender, basting and turning dish twice. Let stand, covered, 5 minutes.

Glossary

Akane. Pronounced ah-CONN-ay. Developed in Japan in 1939. Medium-size, bright red over pale yellow fruit with juicy, white, fine-textured flesh. A slightly tart flavor similar to Jonathan. Available in August and September, particularly in the Northwest. Doesn't store well. Good for eating fresh. Makes a pretty pink sauce when cooked unpeeled and strained.

Braeburn. A chance seedling from New Zealand. Yellow-green with red highlights. Crisp and tangy, pale green flesh. Available in late fall and from the Southern Hemisphere May through August; limited supply. Keeps well. Dual purpose eating/cooking apple that holds its shape when baked.

Cortland. Derived from McIntosh in 1898 in New York. Dark red with green highlights. Tender, juicy, snow-white flesh is slow to brown. Lively tart flavor. Grown primarily in the Northeast and Midwest. An all-purpose apple, ideal for applesauce and salads as well as eating fresh.

Criterion. Chance seedling from near Wapato, Washington; introduced in 1973. Large, Golden Delicious-type apple with smooth, golden green skin often blushed with pink. Sweet firm flesh; juicy. Resists browning. Low acid; add lemon juice when cooking.

Elstar. Bred in Holland in 1955. Golden Delicious crossed with Ingrid Marie. Popular in Europe. Bright red over yellow skin. Aromatic, sweet-tart flavor. Crisp, firm, white flesh. A tangy apple for eating fresh. Retains its flavor when cooked. Excellent for apple pie and sauce.

Empire. Developed in New York in 1966. A cross between McIntosh and Red Delicious. Round with dark red skin, crisp texture, and aromatic, juicy flesh. Keeps well. Primarily available in the Northeast and upper Midwest. All-purpose apple, tends to break down in cooking.

Fuji. Originated in Japan; introduced in 1962. Yellowish green with red highlights, higher color when grown in cooler areas. Low acid; crisp and sweet. Stores well until May. Primarily available in the Northwest and California. Limited supplies. Excellent fresh, loses flavor when cooked.

Gala. Bred in New Zealand in 1965. Related to Golden Delicious. Scarlet stripes over yellow. Royal Gala is a red strain. Fine-textured, yellowish flesh. Distinctive sweet flavor. Available August to December and in the spring from the Southern Hemisphere. Best eaten fresh.

Golden Delicious. Chance seedling found in West Virginia in 1890. Widely grown throughout the world. Ranges from a tart yellow-green to a sweet golden yellow. When the skin is light yellow, the flavor is mild sweet-tart. The firm flesh resists darkening when cut and holds its shape when cooked. Available year-round, nationwide. All-purpose apple with good eating and cooking qualities.

Granny Smith. Originated about 1868 as a chance seedling in New South Wales, Australia. Medium to large. Bright green skin with a slightly yellow undertone when ripe. Crisp, firm texture, juicy, and tart. Available year-round, nationwide. Considered an all-purpose apple. Fine for sauce, but tends to fall apart when baked.

Gravenstein. Probably of German origin, was known in Denmark in 1669. Grown primarily in California and the Northwest. Limited availability. Fairly large apple, greenish yellow splashed with varying degrees of orangey red, depending on the strain. Juicy with a distinctive tart-sweet flavor. All-purpose apple, outstanding for pies and applesauce.

Idared. Originated in Moscow, Idaho, a Jonathan relative, introduced in 1942. Popular in the Northeast. Crimson over yellow-green skin. Fine-textured flesh, juicy, and crisp. Mild, delicate flavor. Stores well. All-purpose, good choice to sauté or use in pies.

Jonagold. Introduced in Geneva, New York, in 1968. A cross between Golden Delicious and Jonathan. Large apple, yellow overlaid with red. Crisp and juicy with a tangy sweet flavor. Rich and complex. Superb in the fall but can become soft when removed from cold storage. All-purpose apple, excellent for eating fresh. Holds its shape when cooked.

Jonathan. Found in New York around 1826. Thought to be a seedling of Esopus Spitzenburg. Medium to small apple, solid red or red stripes over yellow. Moderately tart with tender-crisp, flavorful flesh. Thin skin. All-purpose apple, cooks quickly.

Liberty. Scab-resistant variety bred at Geneva, New York, a Macoun cross; introduced in 1978. Medium-size apple, mostly red skin. White, crisp, and juicy flesh. Tart flavor similar to Spartan and Empire. Keeps well. Excellent fresh.

Macoun. A McIntosh cross; introduced in Geneva, New York, in 1923. Popular in the Northeast. Medium-size apple, dark red over green skin, greenish white flesh. Juicy like McIntosh. Best eaten fresh.

McIntosh. Discovered in Ontario, Canada, about 1800 by John McIntosh. Widely grown in Canada and eastern United States. Many variations. Medium-size, round fruit. Crisp, very juicy with white flesh. Skin somewhat thick. Outstanding for eating fresh. Flavor is good when cooked, but fruit tends to fall apart.

Melrose. A Jonathan-Red Delicious cross from Wooster, Ohio. Introduced in 1944. Large, red splotched over yellow background. Firm, sweet-tart, juicy flesh. Popular in the Midwest. Limited availability. Keeps well in storage. All-purpose apple, makes a full-flavored sauce.

Mutsu. Also called Crispin. A Golden Delicious-Indo cross introduced in Japan in 1948. Large, yellow-green with crisp, coarse flesh. Sweet, spicy flavor. Stores well. All-purpose. Good eaten out-of-hand. Similar to Golden Delicious for cooking.

Newtown Pippin. Called Pippin in California and Oregon. Was popular in Long Island, New York, in 1759. Round, medium-size apple, slightly yellowish green with russeting at the stem end. Cream-colored flesh is crisp and tart but darkens when cut. Good keeper. All-purpose apple, excellent for eating fresh, pies, and general cooking.

Northern Spy. Grown primarily in the Northeast and Great Lakes area. Large apple, bright red over pale yellow. Yellow flesh is tender, juicy, and fairly tart. All-purpose apple, mainly processed into applesauce and pie filling.

Red Delicious. Originated in Iowa. Many strains, ranging from solid burgundy to green with red stripes. White flesh. Tough skin. Small to large. Characteristic five bumps on the blossom end. Crisp and juicy when at its best. Available year-round, nationwide. Best as an eating apple; cooking results in poor texture and flavor.

Rhode Island Greening. A chance seedling from near Newport, Rhode Island, about 1740. Medium to large apple, green to yellowish green skin. Crisp, tart, cream-colored flesh; juicy. Limited availability, mostly in New York, New England, Michigan, and other north-central states. Good for all cooking, particularly pie.

Rome Beauty. Originated in Ohio. Large, round, shiny red apple with greenish white flesh, very firm. Medium tart to sweet. May become mealy late in the season. Good for baking whole; holds shape well.

Spartan. McIntosh cross with Yellow Newtown Pippin. Introduced in 1936 in Summerland, British Columbia, where it is extensively grown. Medium-size apple, mahogany red skin. White, fine-textured flesh. Aromatic, sweet, and juicy. Good for eating fresh and for applesauce.

Stayman. Also called Stayman's Winesap. A Winesap cross found in Kansas in 1875. Deep purplish red skin. White flesh. Rich, mildly tart flavor, tender, and juicy. Available in the mid- and southern Atlantic states. Good for eating fresh and cooking.

Winesap. Originated in New York sometime before 1817. Medium size, round with dark red skin and firm yellow flesh. Sweet, winey flavor. All-purpose apple, good for eating fresh. Retains its flavor in pies and sauces.

York. Also called York Imperial. Originated in York, Pennsylvania, around 1830. Lopsided apple, with warm red over green. Slightly tart. Primarily grown in the mid-Atlantic states. For baking and cooking.

LIST OF RECIPES

TABLE OF EQUIVALENTS

US/UK
oz=ounce
lb=pound
in=inch
ft=foot
tbl=tablespoon
fl oz=fluid ounce
qt=quart

Metric
g=gram
kg=kilogram
mm=millimeter
cm=centimeter
ml=milliliter
l=liter

Weights

US/UK	Metric
1 oz	30 g
2 oz	60 g
3 oz	90 g
4 oz (¼ lb)	125 g
5 oz (⅓ lb)	155 g
6 oz	185 g
7 oz	220 g
8 oz (½ lb)	250 g
10 oz	315 g
12 oz (¾ lb)	375 g
14 oz	440 g
16 oz (1 lb)	500 g
1½ lb	750 g
2 lb	1 kg
3 lb	1.5 kg

Length Measures

⅛ in	3 mm
¼ in	6 mm
½ in	12 mm
1 in	2.5 cm
2 in	5 cm
3 in	7.5 cm
4 in	10 cm
5 in	13 cm
6 in	15 cm
7 in	18 cm
8 in	20 cm
9 in	23 cm
10 in	25 cm
11 in	28 cm
12 in/1 ft	30 cm

Liquids

US	Metric	UK
2 tbl	30 ml	1 fl oz
½ cup	60 ml	2 fl oz
⅓ cup	80 ml	3 fl oz
½ cup	125 ml	4 fl oz
⅔ cup	160 ml	5 fl oz
¾ cup	180 ml	6 fl oz
1 cup	250 ml	8 fl oz
1½ cups	375 ml	12 fl oz
2 cups	500 ml	16 fl oz
4 cups/1 qt	1 liter	32 fl oz

Oven Temperatures

Fahrenheit	Celsius	Gas
250	120	½
275	140	1
300	150	2
325	160	3
350	180	4
375	190	5
400	200	6
425	220	7
450	230	8
475	240	9
500	260	10

TABLE OF EQUIVALENTS

All-Purpose (Plain) Flour/Dried Bread Crumbs/Chopped Nuts

¼ cup	1 oz	30 g
⅓ cup	1½ oz	45 g
½ cup	2 oz	60 g
¾ cup	3 oz	90 g
1 cup	4 oz	125 g
1½ cups	6 oz	185 g
2 cups	8 oz	250 g

White Sugar

¼ cup	2 oz	60 g
⅓ cup	3 oz	90 g
½ cup	4 oz	125 g
¾ cup	6 oz	185 g
1 cup	8 oz	250 g
1½ cups	12 oz	375 g
2 cups	1 lb	500 g

Jam/Honey

2 tbl	2 oz	60 g
¼ cup	3 oz	90 g
½ cup	5 oz	155 g
¾ cup	8 oz	250 g
1 cup	11 oz	345 g

Whole-Wheat (Wholemeal) Flour

3 tbl	1 oz	30 g
½ cup	2 oz	60 g
⅔ cup	3 oz	90 g
1 cup	4 oz	125 g
1¼ cups	5 oz	155 g
1⅔ cups	7 oz	210 g
1¾ cups	8 oz	250 g

Long-Grain Rice/Cornmeal

⅓ cup	2 oz	60 g
½ cup	2½ oz	75 g
¾ cup	4 oz	125 g
1 cup	5 oz	155 g
1½ cups	8 oz	250 g

Grated Parmesan/Romano Cheese

¼ cup	1 oz	30 g
½ cup	2 oz	60 g
¾ cup	3 oz	90 g
1 cup	4 oz	125 g
1⅓ cups	5 oz	155 g
2 cups	7 oz	220 g